A LAWYER'S GUIDE TO ABUNDANCE

BY

MICHAEL MORAN,

ATTORNEY-AT-LAW

the Peppertree Press
Sarasota, Florida

ISBN: 978-1-61493-545-2

Library of Congress Number: 2017912802

Printed March 2018

DEDICATION

*To my wife, Catherine Ann,
who made an abundant life possible.*

ACKNOWLEDGMENT

*Sincere thanks to Julie Ann James
and Peppertree Press.*

TABLE OF CONTENTS

INTRODUCTION

My legal career began in 1987. At that time, I was $54,000.00 in debt, I owned a bed, a TV, $500.00 worth of clothes, and a twelve-year-old beat-up car. I had no connections.

Twenty-seven years later, I was fully retired with over 5.1 million in assets consisting of CDs, stocks, 14 rental properties, and my house, cars, boat, wave-runners, and motorcycles, which I owned free and clear.

I was financially independent. I was also abundant in things that money cannot buy like good health and great relationships. I was happily married to my first and only wife for 25 years and had two terrific children. My health was excellent, I ran marathons and had developed an interest in high altitude climbing, so I had summited peaks in America, Europe, Africa, and South America.

Good Luck!

I accomplished this from humble beginnings: my dad died when I was 18 years old and left a widow, six children, $5,000.00 worth of life insurance, and $40,000.00 of debt and my mother never earned over $12,000.00 per year.

IF I CAN DO IT, SO CAN YOU.

I am no smarter than anyone reading this, but I did study wealth and wealthy people, so the suggestions that follow can make any lawyer (or any person, for that matter) rich. You will need to commit yourself to study money, investments, the stock market, and rental properties. You must avoid debt and learn how to legally minimize your taxes. You will also need to focus on *getting* rich, but not *looking* rich.

I retired when I was 55 years old and in my city we had around 1,200 attorneys. I know of only *one* who voluntarily retired younger than me, and he was 50 years old when he retired. (Many attorneys retire involuntarily, because of poor physical or mental health and simply cannot work anymore.) I asked that 50-year-old retired lawyer how he retired so young and his favorite response was, "I had one wife, one house, and one kid." There is a lot of wisdom in that statement.

As I got older, many of my colleagues, clients, and people I knew would say, "When I am 62 years old, I am going to retire and my wife and I are going to travel and live it up." Unfortunately, most of them would have a heart attack or some kind of health catastrophe and never be able to enjoy their retirement.

If you follow these suggestions, you will retire young enough with enough wealth and health to enjoy the rest of your life.

CHAPTER 1
HOW TO GET A JOB

Law schools are cranking out attorneys in record numbers. Graduates in the top 10% of their class have no problem finding jobs. This book of advice is written for the other 90%.

When I graduated law school back in the Stone Age, you had to write a cover letter and enclose your résumé, mail it, then wait seven to fourteen days for a response. Most of the time, it was a rejection, but occasionally you were granted an interview, which would again take a few days or weeks to schedule. There was generally a second interview and the position was usually given to the attorney with the highest academic credentials. Of course, you can do all this today, but much faster. However, you often get the same result: no job offer.

That is exactly what I did in Tampa, Florida, for several months as I studied for the Bar Exam. However, I was quickly down to my last $100.00.

Out of desperation, I photocopied the Martindale-Hubbell legal directory for Tampa and had 100 of my résumés printed. I then went to the tallest building in downtown Tampa and took the elevator to the top floor. I stood outside the door to every law firm and looked up what area of the law they handled. If they handled personal injury law, I then walked in, introduced myself to the receptionist, and explained I was a recent law school graduate, I was taking the Bar Exam in six weeks, I was looking for a job, and my goal was to be an excellent personal injury lawyer.

I then went to the next law firm, repeated the process and stated I was interested in criminal law, worker's compensation, bankruptcy law, family law, or civil litigation—the area of law did not matter. I was interested and prepared to start immediately! I went to every law firm on the top floor, then went down one floor, and repeated the process.

Surprisingly, about half the time, the receptionist would walk back to speak to her boss and often he would invite me into his office (there were not many female attorneys in the '80s) and we would talk for 15 minutes or so. Several attorneys said they were not hiring, but called a lawyer friend who was looking to hire and sent me over for an interview.

The attorneys seemed to appreciate my cold calling—they could see my demeanor and hear me speak, which you do not get from a written résumé or email. They also seemed to appreciate the gumption of a young guy walking in and asking for a job.

I cold called seventy lawyers/law firms in one day and I had two job offers the first day. The next day my phone was ringing off the hook! I accepted a job with a sole practitioner who handled bankruptcy law, including contested bankruptcy matters and adversary lawsuits in bankruptcy court. I stayed with that attorney for five months until I passed the bar and found a higher paying job handling civil litigation in Sarasota, a city I preferred over Tampa (the commute was terrible in Tampa). I also did not enjoy the repetitive nature of bankruptcy law when I was a new attorney. Ironically, I began handling bankruptcies and contested bankruptcy matters after a ten-year hiatus and enjoyed it immensely the second time around. You never know what area of the law you might enjoy or which office or firm is best for you, so keep an open mind and try them all.

Besides cold calling, a second suggestion is to include a photograph of yourself with your résumé. You do not need a "glam photo"—a passport-size photo will do—just attach it to your résumé. Potential employers want to know what you look like. Years later, as an employer, I would place an ad in the *Florida Bar News* for an associate attorney and I would be flooded with over 100 résumés, sometimes in less than 48 hours. I would have to stop the ad. If I received 100 résumés, maybe one or two would include a photograph. Those always caught my eye and I always interviewed those applicants. I often ended up hiring him or her.

A third suggestion is offer to work for free for a week or two. If you do not have a job, what do you have to lose? You can offer to work free for a week filing, doing legal research, organizing files—whatever needs to be done. The fancy phrase for this is "unpaid internship." I have done this with new attorneys and sometimes I hired them and sometimes I did not. However, I usually ended up paying a stipend of say $15.00 per hour. Even if unpaid, they could put some much needed work experience on their résumé and I would give a positive reference. Once, an attorney that offered to work for free came to me several years later and I hired her.

INCLUDE A PHOTOGRAPH OF YOURSELF WITH YOUR RÉSUMÉ

CHAPTER 2
HOW TO GET
A BETTER JOB

Once you have a job, always do more than you are paid for. Don't be like the person standing in front of the fireplace saying, "Give me more heat and I will give you more wood." Life does not work that way. Sometimes you may feel, "My boss doesn't recognize or appreciate the work I am putting in and I am not being paid enough." In fact, at one point in my career, I felt the same way. Rest assured, however, your boss sees what you are doing and so do other bosses.

Someone is always watching. If you aren't compensated properly where you presently work and you are an "A" employee (meaning you get your work done on time, you show up early and work late, and you are well-prepared for every hearing or trial), someone else will notice you and offer you a job. Don't be too quick to dismiss your prospects where you currently work, because if you are an energized employee, your boss does not want to lose you. Work harder, work more hours, and get good results—the money will come.

What kind of lawyer does an employer want? They want an honest, hard-working, and well-prepared attorney.

Everyone you come in contact with can immediately see your work habits.

What is your appearance? Do you look professional or upon closer examination, do you look unkempt? I recall speaking to many attorneys in courtrooms and in hallways before and after hearings. I would notice stains on their ties or shirts, dirty collars, hair growing out of their ears, and the like. I was speaking with one attorney and I swear his tie looked like a knitted sock he wrapped around his neck! It is hard to concentrate on the words when your eyes are distracted by what they are seeing.

Do you think clients notice that? Or Judges? Of course, they do. Everyone notices everything.

How about being on time? What is that old saying: better three hours early than one minute late. Do you think you impress a judge showing up several minutes late? When you are trying to persuade a person to rule in your favor, you alienate him or her by showing up late. I am proud to say I was late for court only twice in 28 years, once for a flat tire and once because traffic was stopped on the highway because of a fatality. Both judges were understanding, because I had appeared in front of both numerous times and I was always five or ten minutes early for all other hearings and trials.

I once fired an attorney for showing up late for court three times in one month. As an employer, you definitely do not like telephone calls from Judicial Assistants asking where your associate attorney is. Ironically, I was waiting in a different courtroom five years later and that same attorney I fired for being late was again ten minutes late—she came in unprepared and the judge was furious. She had not changed. She did not get it. Is someone else likely to offer that attorney a job? Of course not.

By contrast, if you look professional, your office looks professional, you are on time, prepared, honest, and not afraid to go to court, you will get offers from other law firms. I know, because I have made such offers myself and hired some fine attorneys that way. I have also had fine attorneys hired away from me. The best way to get a better job is to deliver consistently outstanding performance in your present job.

IF YOU LOOK PROFESSIONAL,

YOUR OFFICE LOOKS PROFESSIONAL

CHAPTER 3
DO GOOD WORK
...AND DO IT FAST!

Get the legal work out the door. I was trained with a "72-Hour Rule," which I continued with attorneys that worked for me. This rule mandates that whatever comes in the door goes out again within 72 hours. If someone comes in for a divorce, send that client the proposed divorce petition within 72 hours. If someone comes in with a business dispute, make sure a demand letter goes out within 72 hours. No exceptions. Even if you have to stay late. Even if you're tired and want to go home. Even if the legal document is only 90% correct.

When I was the boss, I instructed all associate attorneys that I would much rather a document go out the door 90% correct than not go out. This sounds counter-intuitive at first, however, clients love speed and they cannot tell if a document is 90% correct or 100% correct, but they *definitely* notice if they have given a lawyer several thousand dollars and do not receive anything in return.

The universe loves speed and so do clients. Clients cannot tell in the beginning if you are a good lawyer, but they definitely notice if you are a slow lawyer. In my career, I acquired between six and ten clients per year who had first been to other attorneys, gave that attorney a large retainer, and yet nothing had been done by that attorney—sometimes for three to four months!

A few years back, a woman came to me and told me she had paid an attorney $4,000.00 three months ago and the attorney had yet to file her divorce petition. I told her if she gave me a $4,000.00 retainer, I guarantee to file her divorce within 48 hours or give her money back. As it turns out, I filed it the same day I was hired. Her divorce was ultimately settled and she has since referred over half a dozen people to me.

Civil litigation and family law is actually very forgiving on amendments and you often amend pleadings anyway, so I found it was more important to get it out the door 90% correct than to not get it out the door.

If you obey the 72-Hour Rule, you will be swamped with clients. Several years ago I hired an associate attorney who was also a Certified Public Accountant. He had impeccable educational credentials from fine universities. However, it was like pulling teeth to get him to get documents out the door. I worked with him over a year trying to speed him up, but ultimately had to replace him. I went through all his files and found three original pleadings in three different cases that were never filed! One was an original Proof of Claim in an estate and fortunately I discovered it with only three days left to file. The claim was for $82,000.00, it was a legitimate claim and it was paid within 30 days of filing. It was signed by the client, notarized and witnessed, but incredibly, never filed with the court.

<u>REMEMBER THE GOLDEN RULE:</u>

GET IT OUT THE DOOR
WITHIN 72 HOURS

CHAPTER 4
CONTINUE TO LEARN
NEW PRACTICE AREAS

If you want to get wealthy, stay in "learning mode" the rest of your life. My firm was 60% civil litigation, but I also handled family law, criminal law, bankruptcy, bankruptcy litigation, and almost every area of the law at one time or another. Some people feel a lawyer should specialize. I disagree.

I found many areas of the law overlap, so if you understand and handle several areas of the law, in my view, it makes you a better lawyer. For instance, many times when collecting a judgment, the defendant will threaten to file bankruptcy. If you know bankruptcy law and understand what the debtor may keep and what will be seized by the trustee, you have a tremendous advantage in civil cases. You can tell the defendant, "Go ahead and file bankruptcy. You can keep your house, but the trustee will seize your vacant lots and your business and your one-half interest in the five acres in North Florida you own. And by the way, we are going to file an adversarial action in bankruptcy court against you and your wife objecting to your discharge, because you transferred assets to your wife and daughter and you have failed to produce the documents that explain what happened to the $60,000.00 you had in the bank six months ago."

When you have that kind of knowledge, it makes you a much better attorney and more valuable to your clients. Moreover, once a client trusts you, they do not want to be referred to a new lawyer at a different firm. In reality, they often never come back! There is also many times an interplay between different areas of the law, especially family law, civil law, and criminal law.

For example, many times in a divorce or family law dispute, the husband or wife threatens to have their spouse arrested for forgery, opening the spouse's mail, and other alleged crimes during a contentious divorce. If you understand criminal law, you know it's not a criminal act to sign a spouse's name to a check, if you have permission. It is done all the time and specifically authorized by the Uniform Commercial Code. Sometimes years later, when a spouse realizes their significant other has a boyfriend or girlfriend, all of a sudden, signing a spouse's name to a check three years earlier is supposedly forgery. If you know criminal law, you understand that is not a criminal offense and can advise your client accordingly, which they appreciate. They also appreciate they do not have to hire a second lawyer to handle their legal issues. Additionally, you earn much more money if you handle for a single client a divorce, a criminal case, a bankruptcy, and then a new will and estate plan. It also benefits the client, since he or she is not hiring four different lawyers.

Another advantage to handling several areas of the law is that it can put food on the table. During the "Great Recession" (what was so "great" about that recession anyway?) from 2008 through 2013, I knew dozens of real estate attorneys who were wandering around looking for work. Many were my friends. There was no real estate work. I offered to teach a few attorney friends how to handle mortgage foreclosure defense (for free). There were no takers. They were all afraid to learn a new area of the law, even when they had an experienced attorney (me) willing to share pleadings and advice for free. Many of those same attorneys found their own houses in foreclosure and I represented several, including a few bankruptcies.

If they had an open mind and a willingness to learn a new area of the law, they would have solved their short-term money problems and helped their career long-term. During the Great Recession, I could not keep up with the work. I had to hire attorneys to keep up. I was willing to devote my time, energy, and brain power to the areas of law that were most in demand at that time and it paid off handsomely. It was beneficial to me, as well as to hundreds of clients whom I helped and for whom I got great results.

One caveat on handling multiple areas of the law: some areas have strict deadlines and requirements, like medical malpractice. Do not take a wrongful death medical malpractice case as your first medical malpractice case. Co-counsel a case like that with an experienced attorney. For areas of the law new to you, start out small and find a mentor. You would be amazed how many experienced attorneys would help you if you simply ask them.

Attorneys that are good in one area of the law are proud of their expertise and love to share their knowledge. Take them to lunch (and buy) and you will be happily surprised.

Keep an open mind. When I started my legal career, I worked for an attorney who received a call from an out-of-state Savings and Loan Bank that was looking for an attorney on the West Coast of Florida to handle admiralty cases. The bank said they could only find one law firm in Tampa, but their legal fees were extremely high. My boss told the bank he did not handle admiralty cases, but he was willing to educate himself at no charge to the bank. They agreed and sent the first case, a $300,000.00 First Preferred Ship Mortgage foreclosure. He researched the law, modified pleadings he discovered in Federal Court and earned a $5,000.00 fee (which was a large fee 30 years ago). The bank was pleased, because the Tampa firm they previously used charged $15,000.00 for the same work.

We made a few mistakes in the beginning, but got better and better over time. I eventually took over the admiralty cases and we expanded to handling vessel repossessions in numerous states and the Caribbean and ultimately handled over 50 admiralty cases, earning hundreds of thousands of dollars. It was good for the bank and good for us and came about because my boss at the time had a willingness to learn a new area of the law.

Be a problem solver. You have heard phrases like, "Be a self-starter" and "Be a problem solver" for years, so you may have tuned them out. These are old clichés, but contain a lot of wisdom. From a client's standpoint, they are enormous. People come to lawyers because they have a problem. People will happily pay a lot of money for someone to solve their problems. I always told attorneys working for me to "solve the problem and solve it as quickly and inexpensively as possible." Clients love that. If you can only solve small problems, you will not be paid much.

IF YOU CAN SOLVE BIG PROBLEMS, YOU WILL BE PAID BIG MONEY.

Welcome problems and try to solve more complex problems as you advance in your career. Some lawyers are not problem solvers and do the exact opposite. They milk a case or are obstructive on every issue. That type of mindset is not good for clients or lawyers. If you want a thriving law firm, develop the mindset of a problem solver.

Finally, be honest—even if you have bad news. If you make a mistake, make it good for free. Clients love honest, straightforward lawyers.

Once a man came to me for a free consultation after his divorce trial. He had gotten a bad result in his divorce and he was considering an appeal. I read the final judgment carefully and we went over the facts in detail. I told him I would handle his appeal, but it will likely cost $6,000.00 to $10,000.00. I also advised him that he is probably wasting his money and time, because a trial judge is given great discretion in family law cases. He thanked me for my time and said he would let me know.

I did not see him again for two years, when he brought me a completely different business legal matter. I asked him if he had ever appealed his divorce and he said no. He told me he consulted five other attorneys and every single one recommended he appeal. I was the only one that told him it was probably a waste of money. He appreciated my advice and wanted to use me for all his legal needs. He had a successful business and I handled his legal needs for decades.

IF HONESTY DID NOT EXIST, INVENTING IT WOULD BE THE QUICKEST WAY TO GET RICH.

CHAPTER 5
GETTING PAID

Doing quality legal work is half the job. The second part is getting paid. Clients do not like to pay when they lose and some do not like to pay when they win! However, if you provide quality legal services at a fair price, you are destined for wealth, if you follow a few simple rules.

RULE 1

At the outset, clearly explain to clients what you charge and confirm it in writing. It does not need to be a five-page contract, but you should have a simple email or letter explaining your fees, which the client should countersign.

RULE 2

Avoid flat fees and handle legal matters hourly. Even after twenty years, it is difficult to predict how long a matter will take. The big unknown is the other party and the other party's attorney (and sometimes your own client). Some clients will "work you to death," if you have committed to a legal task for a flat fee. I have handled cases that settled in the first two weeks that I thought would require two years of pre-trial wrangling and an eight-day jury trial. I have also handled what I thought was a small dispute that would be resolved in a month that took years of pre-trial hearings, a jury trial, and then an appeal. You never know.

If you agree to handle cases hourly, there are no arguments with clients. Early in my career, I made the mistake of agreeing to handle a small claims case for a flat fee of $1,300.00 (the dispute involved $4,200.00). What I did not anticipate was the defendant avoiding service of process for nine months; conducting two hearings to extend the time to serve the defendant; the pretrial conference being continued three times; and when we finally got to trial, running out of time and having to come back four weeks later for another four hours to conclude the trial! I ended up earning about $20.00 per hour on that flat fee case.

RULE 3

Invoice at least monthly. I remember an older lawyer telling me, "Legal invoicing is an art, as well as a science." I did not understand that at the time, but years later I appreciated the wisdom. If you get a good result, send out a bill immediately while the client is in a good mood. Do *not* wait several weeks to invoice. Conversely, if a client just paid you $4,000.00 on a delinquent invoice, do not send him another invoice a few days later. Wait a few weeks, so the client does not feel you are only interested in money.

RULE 4

Do not put your name on a file without a retainer. Never. Ever. I learned this lesson several times the hard way. I remember a client came to me and said his former business partner was moving to Utah that evening and had to be served with a lawsuit regarding $90,000.00 that was supposedly owed to my client. I told the client I needed a $2,000.00 retainer and $300.00 for costs (this was 25 years ago). He said that was not a problem. He would just get his checkbook from home and give it to me the next time he came in. (Mistake Number 1). I spent all day preparing the lawsuit, the summons, the cover sheet, and arranging for expedited service on the defendant. I unwisely filed the suit before the client brought in the retainer. (Mistake Number 2). Over the next several days, I heard excuse after excuse, but the $2,300.00 never arrived. Fifteen days later, the defendant answered the lawsuit and filed a counterclaim with three promissory notes (in default) signed by my client. Believe it or not, I never received a dime from the client and he never even reimbursed the filing fee or expedited service fee! A lesson learned the hard way. Six months later, I withdrew from the case.

On another occasion (not yet learning my lesson), a wife came to see me and told me her husband had been arrested on felony charges in reference to a dispute involving a leased copier. The wife begged me to represent her husband and get him out of jail and the husband supposedly had money in a safe to pay me. The wife had her three young daughters with her in my office and they all were crying. I made the mistake of putting my name on the felony file without a retainer. (I do not know why I did not simply ask the wife to get the safe combination from her husband to pay the retainer.) I filed the necessary paperwork to have bail reduced and the hearing ten days later was successful, but the husband never paid me when he got out of jail. He said he had to use the money to pay delinquent bills as a result of the 14 days he spent in jail. I told him his most important bill is the one he owes me. The husband said he owned a vacant lot in Orlando worth about $25,000.00 and he would give me a mortgage on the lot to make sure I got paid. I agreed and my partner at the time prepared the mortgage and the client signed it and it was recorded. Six months later, I had all criminal charges dismissed, but the client left town with no forwarding address. No worries, I thought, we will simply foreclose to collect our fee. We filed the foreclosure suit only to discover he gave us a fraudulent deed. He had already sold that lot. I never got paid a dime for over $12,000.00 of legal work.

To be sure, you should do some legal work for free. It is required by the Florida Bar and it is also good Karma. However, that should be the agreement up front—not by default. Speaking of free legal services, I always met with potential clients for a half hour for free for over 25 years and never regretted that policy. I found a free initial consultation benefitted not only the client, but me as well. We could both observe each other's demeanor and if the legal matter involved a document, we could look it over together. I could decide if I felt I could help that person and give an estimate of what I thought it would cost and the likely outcome.

Sometimes I could tell immediately the potential client had unreasonable expectations and I would often decline to handle a legal matter because I felt there was little chance of getting the outcome the client was expecting. By asking questions, I could figure out what the client wanted and if I would be able to deliver that result. I found a half-hour free initial consultation to be a win/win.

Another shift in my behavior over the years was how I approached retainers and clients hiring me. In the beginning of my career, I used high pressure and, after the initial meeting, I would urge the client to hire me immediately so I could get started and I would often demand an immediate decision. It worked some of the time.

In the last fifteen years of my career, I did the exact opposite: After the initial (free) meeting, I told the client, for example, I would need a $2,500.00 retainer and I charge $250.00 per hour. I would tell the client to go home and sleep on it, discuss it with their spouse and feel free to interview other attorneys. About 90% would come back with a retainer and it would start the relationship off on a good note. I made much more money being low key.

RULE 5

If a potential client comes in with a new lawsuit and they do not leave a retainer, do not let them leave the lawsuit with you. Do not make a copy. Explain you would be honored to be their lawyer, but need a retainer to put your name on their court file. Explain that again as you walk them to the door and be very clear that you are *not* their lawyer until they bring in a retainer. If it was the nineteenth day to respond to a lawsuit, I would explain they should put in the court file a written request for an additional ten days to hire a lawyer and send a copy to the plaintiff's lawyer.

Do not put your name on any court file without a retainer, unless you are taking the case pro-bono. If the court case is out of town, get a larger retainer than you usually require, because you do not know how many car or plane trips it will require.

Be wary and very selective on handling contingent cases. Just as you should avoid flat fees, you should avoid handling business disputes on a contingent basis (at least at the beginning of your career). When the prospective client is trying to talk you into handling his civil case for one-third, they never tell you the bad parts. They make it sound like easy money, but my experience was the exact opposite. There were often counterclaims and rarely did the cases settle.

Moreover, even when we won a trial, collection was often difficult. Be selective on handling civil cases contingently or you may end up spending a lot of hours for no fee.

I did, however, handle many cases on a "modified-contingent basis," whereby the client put some money up front, but got a credit on the back end, if there was a recovery. For example, say the client felt they were owed $100,000.00 over a business dispute. I would sometimes tell the client I will handle their dispute for 30% of what I recovered, but they would have to pay a $5,000.00 non-refundable retainer up-front, but would be credited that $5,000.00 out of any recovery. If we won $100,000.00, my fee would be $30,000.00 less the $5,000.00 paid up-front, so I would receive $25,000.00 and the client would receive $75,000.00. If we recovered only $30,000.00, I would receive

30% of $30,000.00 or $9,000.00, less the $5,000.00 paid up-front, or $4,000.00, and the client would receive $26,000.00. If we lost, I would receive nothing, the client would receive nothing and the $5,000.00 would not be returned.

Under all scenarios, the client paid costs (filing fee, court reporters, etc.). Depending upon the amount involved, sometimes my percentage was 25%, 20%, or even 15%. I explained I had confidence in my abilities and I was willing to take some risk, but not all the risk. I found that clients that had confidence in their case did not mind putting money up front with the understanding they would get a credit on the back end. In fact, it was like a litmus test.

I never lost a case where the client agreed to a modified contingent case. Clients that did not have confidence in their case never came back. If you handle cases on a modified contingent basis, it must be in writing and countersigned by the client. In certain business disputes, handling them on a modified contingent basis can be a win/win for you and the client.

CHAPTER 6
HIRING ASSOCIATE ATTORNEYS

I have worked in large law firms and as a sole practitioner. Bigger is not always better. At one firm, I remember how proud I was when I was promoted from associate attorney to partner. However, my happiness diminished over the next several months as I sat in on budget meetings and realized the tremendous overhead for a law firm with 25 employees. In fact, all expenses and employees had to be paid before the partners. At one point, I went three months and only received $1,000.00 over that time.

One evening I went home and told my wife, I am supporting 17 families, but not my own—something is wrong with this picture. Eventually, another hard-working attorney and I left and formed our own law firm and I never missed a paycheck again. Thereafter, I always kept my overhead low and employees to a minimum. It was a messy dissolution of the former firm, but a valuable lesson learned.

I also learned to hire employees that could fill more than one role. For example, I would hire a bookkeeper that was also willing to act as receptionist and perhaps do some filing and light typing. I would hire a legal secretary that was not opposed to acting as an occasional courier and making telephone calls to clients to collect delinquent invoices. It worked.

Another thing I did was hire associate attorneys at a base salary and a monthly bonus based upon how much money that attorney brought in the previous month.

I usually hired attorneys at a base salary of $30,000.00 per year and a monthly bonus between zero and $10,000.00 per month.

Yes, you are reading that right: $30,000.00 per year base salary. Was it hard to find attorneys? Not at all. I always had more willing applicants than positions available. I came up with this compensation structure as a result of hiring several dud attorneys. I previously hired some attorneys at a starting salary of $60,000.00 to $70,000.00 per year. By some estimates, an associate attorney must bring in twice their salary for the firm to "break even" on that attorney.

The firm only makes a profit on what that attorney brings in over that amount. I had previously hired attorneys that did not even bring in enough revenue to cover their own salary, let alone their secretary's or any money towards overhead.

I found by hiring associate attorneys at a very modest base salary, if it turned out anyone was a dud, it did not cost me very much. If it turned out someone was a great attorney, I was happy to pay monthly bonuses of $5,000.00 or even over $8,000.00. It was a win/win.

This compensation structure also involved the associate attorney to ensure that clients were paying their invoices for services rendered. By the way, the monthly bonus paid to the associate attorney was based upon income brought in the previous month (not hours billed). The monthly bonus ranged from 20% to 30% of monies brought in depending upon length of employment.

A final benefit of this compensation package was the type of person it attracted—attorneys with courage and confidence in their abilities and a willingness to work hard—in other words, "hungry" attorneys. Those were the ones I wanted. Much like a salesman on straight commission, you either produced or received very little income. I used this compensation structure for almost twenty years and it worked like a charm for me and the attorneys that produced.

You might ask what is the difference between a "dud attorney" and a good attorney? A dud attorney comes in late and usually leaves early. He or she is generally pessimistic and a "downer" to be around. They typically put in minimum effort to prepare for a hearing or trial. They get their best ideas on the walk back from the courthouse. They are slow and often do not respond to telephone calls or e-mails for days—sometimes not at all. They are easy to recognize.

A good attorney is also easy to recognize: They are prompt, well-prepared, happy, out-going, and optimistic about the outcome of any legal matter. They have courage. They are not afraid to try cases. They do not settle cases just to get rid of them. They are upbeat and fun to be around and they have interests outside the law. Clients want to hire them and when clients see how hard they are working for them, they want to pay them. And they win! Not always, but most of the time. Clients like winners and want to be around them and hire them.

People also like honest lawyers that are not afraid. Good lawyers are easy to recognize, but unfortunately, they are rare. However, if you use a compensation system similar to the one I described, you are likely to hire and retain good lawyers and if a "dud" slips through the cracks, it will not cost too much.

PEOPLE LIKE HONEST LAWYERS THAT ARE NOT AFRAID

CHAPTER 7
COLLECTION PROCEDURES

You must have a procedure in place (preferably in writing) that everyone in the office follows to collect delinquent invoices. My policy was as follows:

1. When an invoice was fifteen days overdue, I had my bookkeeper call the client (if you do not have a full-time bookkeeper, have your secretary or receptionist call or even, do it yourself). Ask if they received the invoice and whether they mailed a check. In a few instances, the clients moved or the invoice was mailed to an incorrect address.

2. Next, if we did not receive payment within the next five days, we sent a letter informing the client that the firm provides quality legal services and we expect our clients to pay their invoices in a timely manner. A sample letter can be found in the Appendix.

3. If payment was not received within five days, we sent a stronger letter advising the client we have stopped all work on their case and explaining the office has expenses, like any other business and could not continue if the client did not pay. (See Appendix).

4. If payment was not received within five days, we sent one final letter advising the client that if payment

was not received within ten days, we would have no alternative but to file a Motion to Withdraw and recommend the client retain another attorney to handle their case and have their new attorney file a Notice of Appearance in their case within the next ten days. (See Appendix).

This last letter also explained that we must obtain a court order to withdraw as their attorney and once that is granted, they will be representing themselves and the other side can win in as little as twenty-five days if the suit is not properly handled. The final letter also explained that if the other side wins, they can do mean things like garnish their bank accounts, seize vehicles, and non-exempt assets. The final letter worked about 80% of the time and I often worked out payment plans with clients and explained if they paid a reasonable amount every month, I could pay my expenses and continue as their attorney.

If not, I withdrew from their case, so I could be available in the office for the new client who *was* willing to pay.

I would tell my clients a quote I read somewhere that said: "I can go to court on your behalf and butt heads with the other party, the other lawyer, and sometimes the judge and not get paid—or I could go to the beach with my family and not get paid. Which would you choose?" It really made clients think and caused many to rethink the situation and pay.

I found most clients felt they would eventually pay me at some unspecified time in the future. We had a friendly relationship, so they thought I could wait to be paid. However, "The road to hell is paved with good intentions." I would explain that I cannot pay my employees or rent with good intentions, so this statement usually resulted in payment.

Over the years, we also developed standard replies to client excuses for not paying their invoice. If the client told my bookkeeper they wanted to discuss an item on the invoice with me, my bookkeeper automatically told them to skip that item, pay the rest of the invoice, and she would discuss that item with me. (Some clients would use one item to try to avoid paying the entire bill.)

Many times, if the client paid $1,850.00 on a $2,000.00 invoice, I would simply write off the difference as a courtesy discount. Some clients would say they have a check sitting on their desk, but have been too busy to mail it or drop it off at our office. My bookkeeper would automatically say no problem, what is the address and she will be there in a half hour to pick up the check.

When she returned, I would give her an extra $50.00 to $100.00 for picking up the check. If she was picking up a $2,500.00 check, I did not care if it took a half a day. Some clients would say they need to speak to me about their case before they paid their bill. My bookkeeper would automatically say I do not give additional legal advice until the invoice for the past legal advice is paid. These standard responses from my bookkeeper resulted in money coming in fast and not wasting hours each day on never-ending telephone calls regarding invoices, which could not be billed. Invariably, questions about their case were ones that had been asked and answered many times previously. I was also no longer staying at the office until 7:00 p.m. returning telephone calls, but instead was home with my family.

Do not sue former clients, except in the rarest of circumstances. It often results in a Florida Bar Complaint, even if you won the underlying suit. (The client complaint: you should have won the suit faster or charged less!) Suing your former client also often triggers a counterclaim, which you then have to report to your Professional Liability Carrier (even if it is frivolous). I found a much better strategy is to have a "drop dead" limit of say $1,500.00 or $2,000.00. When a client is delinquent and reaches that number, stop all work, start the letters and/or emails mentioned previously mentioned and eventually withdraw if they do not pay. Continue to invoice the former client, but do not file suit—chalk it up as another lesson learned.

I've dealt with many highly stressed people. Many had been arrested for the first time, some discovered their spouse was having an affair, or their business partner had taken off with all the assets. Quite a few of these people were angry at me, sometimes yelling at me and furious that they had to pay legal fees on top of everything else they were dealing with.

It took years for me to figure it out, but I eventually learned to explain that whatever happened to them before I met them, I did not do. I calmly explained that I am not sure why they are angry with me, because I am 100% sure I did not cause their difficulties, since I did not even know them. I would then explain I am happy to be their attorney or continue as their attorney as long as we are on the same side, but I will not fight or argue with my own client. I would explain I did not mind fighting the other party, their lawyer and sometimes the judge, but I was not going to fight my own client. It worked 100% of the time.

CHAPTER 8
HANDLING STRESS

When I was a young lawyer, a senior attorney I worked for often said, "The practice of law is 90% psychology." I did not agree with the statement at the time, but 30 years later, I agree completely. You have to develop techniques for dealing with clients, other attorneys and the day-to-day hassles of running a law firm if you want abundance in your practice and your life.

My solution was two-fold: first, I vowed to prepare carefully and do the best I could and not concern myself with the outcome. Becoming detached from the outcome is definitely easier said than done and it took me about six years to control my mind to that point, but it can be accomplished. Ironically, when I finally detached myself from the outcome, I began getting better outcomes. There are many paradoxes in life and that is one of them.

Second, I quit drinking alcohol and started exercising. In the first five years as a lawyer, I had a heavy calendar including a half dozen jury trials per year, so I found myself working 60 to 70 hours per week and going to happy hour on Thursdays and Fridays and drinking more and more, including weekends, when I did not have a trial Monday morning. The legal profession has a high suicide and alcoholism rate. I did not become suicidal, but I definitely began drinking more. A recent study suggests 26% of male attorneys and 16% of female attorneys will develop alcoholism by the end of their careers. After six years as an attorney and after a particularly drunken Saturday night, I decided to stop drinking. I had a wife and two-year-old daughter and I knew my wife was tired of my drinking. I reached a point where I knew I had to quit drinking.

However, I could not imagine a future that did not involve alcohol. I missed alcohol terribly for about six months. I was so used to drinking while doing certain activities like boating, waterskiing, going to football games, parties and the like. I realized I had been drinking since I was 18 years old, but always maintained high grades in college and law school and alcohol had slowly but surely become a big part of my life. Miraculously, after about six months, all desire for alcohol went away. I am glad I quit when I did, because had I waited another five years, I doubt I would have been able to quit. I have not had even a sip of champagne in over twenty-three years. My marriage improved dramatically, my law firm improved dramatically, my memory, my appearance, my patience, and my demeanor all improved and I was a much better lawyer and person.

Alcohol can zap you in many ways. The obvious ways like DUI and domestic violence, but less obvious ways like divorce, business failures, and bad decision-making, both personal and business. Ironically, alcohol created a lot of legal work for me: hundreds of DUIs, divorces, business failures, and problems caused by clouded, poor decisions as a result of drinking.

As time went on, my drinking friends slowly drifted away and I developed new friends. I can honestly say I have more fun in life now without alcohol than when I was drinking. I was not a raging alcoholic or getting arrested, but I was on my way. In sobriety, I found peace and courage. What had frightened me no longer did. Sadly, I have seen dozens of lawyers ruin their careers and lives with drinking and drugs. Be careful or you may become one of them.

THE LEGAL PROFESSION HAS A HIGH SUICIDE AND ALCOHOLISM RATE…

… I DECIDED TO STOP DRINKING

CHAPTER 9
DO NOT OVERWORK

Overwork can cripple you and take all the fun out of life. I only worked two days per week in my last four years as an attorney (Monday and Wednesday). Paradoxically, (again) I made more money working two days per week than when I worked five or six days per week earlier in my career.

Of course I had more experience, but I concluded there were two reasons I was making more money working less hours: First, I did not tolerate clients that did not pay. There simply was no time for non-paying clients. Second, clients were more anxious to hire me. My schedule was booked about fourteen days out at the end of my career. My secretary would explain to clients if they wanted an appointment with me (instead of with an associate attorney), it would be two weeks out. My secretary would explain we understand some legal matters cannot wait fourteen days and feel free to hire another attorney. Surprisingly, about 80% were willing to wait two weeks and they were invariably good payers.

It took about six years to get down to two days per week. I started by taking every Friday off and after eighteen months, I took off Thursday and Friday. Then after another eighteen months, Tuesday, Thursday, and Friday. There were occasions when I had to work one of those days like a jury trial or a bench trial that ran over, but that was usually only four to five times per year. It takes a real shift in your thinking to take week days off every week. It is very tempting to want to make more money, especially if you have a busy practice. You must have other hobbies and interests, because you must reach a point where time is more valuable than money. It is hard to conclude, "I have enough money."

The second thing I changed when I was working two days per week is that I became much more discerning about the cases I handled. Not to sound snobbish, but if it did not involve over $5,000.00, I would encourage people to use the small claims process. I avoided smaller legal disputes, because I found it was not fair to the client to charge $2,500.00 when the dispute involves $3,000.00.

BY DECLINING SMALL CASES,

I WAS READY AND AVAILABLE TO

HANDLE LARGE ONES.

CHAPTER 10
LEGAL WAR STORIES

In my legal career, I successfully prosecuted and defended multimillion-dollar cases in courtrooms throughout Florida.

I handled everything from small claims cases up to oral arguments before the Florida Supreme Court—winning many of these comprehensive cases. I conducted bench and jury trials and handled appeals in both state and federal courts. I defended criminal cases, from misdemeanors to first-degree felonies. Having done all this, I came to a strange conclusion: people take losing their liberty better then losing their money. As strange as it sounds, handling criminal cases where the negotiated plea was several years in the Department of Corrections, clients were generally satisfied with the process and the result. (When there is a very strong criminal case with almost no chance of a Not Guilty verdict, the only thing you usually accomplish by going to trial is to increase the punishment).

By contrast, I handled disputes that sometimes involved less than a thousand dollars, but generated tremendous anger, bitterness, and hatred. Often, the litigants hated the opposing party, the other attorney, me, the judge—everybody— even if they won the case. As crazy as it sounds, I saw this phenomenon numerous times over the years and concluded that people value their money more than their freedom!

COW'S EAR

An interesting case I handled involved a trucker driving a semi-trailer truck packed with a full load of tomatoes. One foggy morning at 5:00 a.m. on a two-lane road in Manatee County, Florida, the trucker came around a bend going 55 mph, only to discover a cow in the middle of the road, which resulted in a violent collision.

The semi flipped on its side and the trucker (who was not wearing his seat belt) went through the front windshield and was knocked unconscious. The trailer split open and tomatoes were all over the road. The semi-trailer truck was totaled—a complete loss.

Another trucker approached the scene from the opposite direction and managed to stop his rig before he ran over the first trucker lying in the middle of the road. An ambulance was called and the first trucker was hospitalized for nearly a month. Before leaving the scene, however, the Good Samaritan trucker located the cow's head and found a tag stapled to the its ear. He used his knife to cut off the cow's ear and stuffed it into the unconscious trucker's shirt pocket. When the trucker was released from the hospital, he was given the clothing he was wearing at the time of the accident. The cow's ear was still in his shirt pocket. A few weeks later, the trucker somehow found me, came to my office, and plunked the cow's wrinkled, dried-out ear on my desk. We were able to track down the owner of the cow by that ear tag. The farm owner initially denied having any cows escape the pasture or losing any cows, but later, after we confirmed ownership through veterinary records, admitted his cow had gotten loose. We later settled the case shortly before trial. Talk about making a silk purse out of a cow's ear!!!

ILLITERATE

Although I handled many high-dollar cases, one of my most memorable involved only $6,500.00. A 78-year-old gentleman came to me and said he had been paying on a used pickup truck for many years, but the amount he owed did not seem to be decreasing. He wondered if his debt would be paid off before he died. I studied his financing agreement carefully and discovered he was paying 34% interest. Auto finance companies are bound by a statute that is a complicated formula based upon the age of a vehicle at the time of financing. I did the math and, as it turns out, the finance company (a well-known national company) was charging 2.7% too much interest—a very lopsided contract in favor of the financing company. When I asked the client why he signed the contract, he told me he could not read. I wrote a demand letter to the finance company explaining the math, pointing out they had charged a usurious rate of interest and demanded that the original title be stamped "Paid in Full" and all monies paid on the used truck be refunded. Incredibly, about ten days later, I received an envelope (no letter) containing the original title stamped "Paid in Full" and a $6,500.00 cashier's check! I asked the client to come in and I showed him the original title and cashier's check. He was so happy he started crying. He told me all he wanted was his truck title and he insisted I keep the $6,500.00 cashier's check. I told him absolutely not as I had worked only one hour on his case—the check was his. He was crying so hard he could barely speak. I often think of that case and it makes me happy. Incidentally, about four months later, I received another $6,500.00 cashier's check from the same auto finance company. Again, no cover letter. I sent it back. You can use the power of the law to help poor people from being financially abused.

I had another client that could not read. I represented him for over a year before his jury trial, which was when I discovered his handicap. The case involved a boundary dispute. He had purchased a house with an adjoining vacant lot, but when he went to build a house on the lot for his mother, he discovered his house jutted over the lot line and the county would not issue a building permit. We found out the seller had tried to get a building permit eight years earlier, but had been refused for the same reason. We asked the seller to rescind the transaction or at least refund some of the purchase price, because of the unbuildable lot. He refused. We filed suit and after one year of pre-trial wrangling, we had a jury trial. During the trial, the other attorney was questioning my client about a specific paragraph in the contract. The attorney asked my client if he had read that paragraph. My client said no, he had not. The attorney asked him why not. He said he couldn't read. I was stunned, because I had written him dozens of letters and he always responded. However, he had family members help him write those letters. Then I remembered how he always had a family member with him when he came to my office. As it turns out, his inability to read did not hurt us and we won the case.

Another case underscored how much we all impact one another's lives. A divorced mother came to me with her 17-year-old son who had a lawsuit filed against him for breach of a business lease, seeking rent of over $30,000.00, plus attorney's fees. The boy was a child prodigy and had started several businesses at a young age, He had leased retail space, but that business failed, so he was unable to pay the rent. They did not have much money and were both very upset and worried about the lawsuit. I noticed the lease was only signed by the son. I filed a Motion to Dismiss and a request for attorney's fees as a 17-year-old boy does not have the legal capacity to enter into a contract. The landlord's attorney dismissed the suit a few days later. About ten years later, I received a letter from that young man explaining he was so impressed by the way I handled that lawsuit that he decided on the spot to become an attorney himself. He graduated college with good grades, was accepted into an excellent law school, graduated, and passed the bar. He now works at a big law firm. One never knows how our actions affect others and the ripple effect we may have on other's lives.

ACT OF DAVID

A woman called me asking if I could prepare an "Act of David" for her. I confessed I had never heard of such a document. Upon further questioning, it turns out her beater car broke down on the side of the highway and she left it there for a week, It was eventually towed and sat in the storage yard for several weeks. The towing company wanted $700.00 to release the car. It was only worth $500.00. The towing company said if she gave them an Act of David, they would keep the car and she would owe no money. I called the towing company—what they actually wanted was an "Affidavit" that she was releasing any interest in the car!

THE TRUTH PREVAILS

A man came to me with a demand letter in his hand from another attorney demanding $640,000.00. It turns out my client borrowed $400,000.00 from a wealthy friend, which was secured by a mortgage on my client's home. According to my client, he and his friend had a verbal agreement that this was supposed to be an interest-free loan. However, the written mortgage said the interest was 10%. It had been six years since the money was lent and my client had never made a payment. I told the gentleman there is a five-year statute of limitations in Florida on written instruments and this debt was time-barred, so he did not have to pay anything.

He told me he did not care about the statute of limitations, because he now had the $400,000.00 originally lent and wanted to pay the full amount and obtain a satisfaction of mortgage. I told him that was his choice, so I wrote the other attorney explaining the debt was time-barred, but my client was still willing to pay the original $400,000.00 lent. The other attorney ignored my letter and filed suit seeking $400,000.00, plus $240,000.00 in interest. However, we won the case and obtained a court order several months later that the debt was time-barred. Incredibly, even after winning the case, my client still wanted to repay the $400,000.00. We did and the lender was only too happy to accept the $400,000.00. Honesty is the best policy.

JUDICIAL RESTRAINT

I have seen many people put in jail and over a dozen held in contempt of court and put in jail in the middle of hearings and trials. However, I handled a divorce where I was amazed at the judicial restraint possessed by one judge. I was representing the wife and they had a five-year-old son. The father had walked out two years earlier and since then, had not seen his son (or paid child support). When we served the husband with the divorce papers, the judge scheduled a hearing, because the husband wanted to have overnight visitations with his son every other weekend, which was standard at the time. We opposed this, because the husband would not disclose where he was living and we thought he would flee with his son. During the hearing, the husband became very agitated and started swearing and making veiled threats. The bailiffs were ready to take the husband into custody. I was amazed as the judge calmly explained he was implementing a schedule to reintroduce the father into the son's life, but it would start out gradually with supervised visitations. If the husband consistently maintained contact with his son, he would eventually have a normal shared parenting relationship with him. The husband calmed down and instead of litigation and acrimony, we settled the case a few months later and the father has regularly seen his son and paid child support.

CHAPTER 11
SAVE YOUR WALNUTS

So far, you are doing good work, fast, and at a fair price. So, how do you get wealthy? First, start *saving*. Until you get into the habit of saving and make it a lifelong habit, you will never get wealthy.

SAVE SOME MONEY
OUT OF EVERY PAYCHECK

My first boss' wife took me aside one day and said I should get into the habit of saving some money out of every paycheck I receive. I followed that advice and started saving $20.00 every Friday which I increased over time. I still remember when I had saved $10,000.00. It felt great to have that financial security. I never touched that money and kept adding to it and eventually it turned into over half a million dollars.

Many things in life are simple, but not easy (like saving money, losing weight, and staying in shape). If you do not develop the savings habit, you will never get wealthy. We are creatures of habit and saving can become fun. You will develop either good or bad habits over time. Develop good habits *early* and stay with them.

CHAPTER 12
RETIREMENT ACCOUNTS

Start a tax-advantaged retirement plan and fund it aggressively with stocks. I used a SEP-IRA, because it was simple and you could put in large amounts (sometimes $40,000.00 per year, depending upon your gross income). I also taught myself about investing in stocks after I lost over $20,000.00 listening to "hot tips" from stockbrokers and friends at cocktail parties. I eventually read over a hundred books on investing and still read them today.

For the last ten years I have been buying the same stocks Warren Buffet buys—stocks like American Express, Coca-Cola, Proctor & Gamble and Wells Fargo Bank—I plan to hold them at least twenty years. If these stocks are good enough for the second richest man in America, they are good enough for me. A "Buy and Hold" strategy minimizes commissions, taxes, and paperwork and it frees up time for other pleasures. You can use a 401K, a Roth IRA, or a traditional IRA, but fund a retirement plan.

Educate yourself on the pros and cons of each, but get in the habit of putting at least $500.00 to $1,000.00 per month into a retirement account for you and your spouse.

If you can only start with $200.00 per month, start anyway. If you make some mistakes with investments, do not worry.

Be skeptical of recommendations from stockbrokers and financial planners. They often recommend investments with huge commissions. I learned the hard way not to invest in companies I have never heard of before. I like to buy stock in companies I use, like ketchup, cereal, and consumer products. I have made mistakes in picking investments, but that is part of the learning curve.

At one point, I hired a financial expert for $5,000.00 per year and he would tell me what stock to purchase or which stock to sell and when to cash out of that position. After one year, I made a modest profit of 6% on the investments, but after deducting his $5,000.00 fee, I lost money. It was also a nightmare to list all those stock transactions on my tax return and pay taxes on the gains. I never did it again. I would have been much better off simply investing in an index fund. Buy and Hold has worked for me.

CHAPTER 13
REAL ESTATE INVESTMENTS

Many years ago, I was talking with an older attorney and he told me, "Make sure you do something one day per week that is not related to the law or you'll be working until you are 65." I followed that advice and began investing in real estate. Real estate has several advantages many investments do not:

- First, legal tax savings. If you have a high income or even a medium income as a W-2 employee, you can legally reduce your taxes. You can pay large amounts to the government in taxes or invest that same money in real estate for your long-term wealth.

- You get depreciation (paper losses) and anything you buy for the rental, you can legally deduct: ladders, compressors, tools, paint, lawn mowers, and vehicles. As long as they are used for the rental, they are legally deductible.

- Moreover, real estate almost always appreciates over time, but you need a long-term perspective like fifteen to thirty years.

- Finally, even if the property is break even on cash flow, eventually you can raise rents and the tenant is paying off the mortgage. My wife and I invested in single family homes and eventually became wealthy, one house at a time.

Do not try to get rich fast

Do not try to get rich fast. It works maybe one time out of a thousand. In fact, when I tried to get rich fast, I lost money every time. Get rich slowly. The time passes anyhow.

Our first rental property was also the first home my wife and I purchased and had lived in six years. By then, we had two children and needed a bigger home. We found a larger one, but instead of selling our first home, we rented it out.

It was a very easy transition into the rental business. No need to get a mortgage for a rental property—simply continue to make the mortgage payments. We made lots of mistakes learning the rental business and we have had some bad tenants, but we learned.

We have had surprisingly few evictions over the last twenty years. We learned to screen tenants carefully. If a prospective tenant asked if they could pay half the security deposit now and half in sixty days, we knew that tenant had money troubles. If the tenant was desperate for a place to rent, we learned that such a person was likely desperate in many other areas of life, so chose not to deal with such persons.

We learned to tell good prospective tenants up front. There are only two things we do not like:

- Tenants calling us with stupid requests
- The rent not being in our mailbox on the first of each month

We fix the items a landlord is supposed to fix and we are honest with tenants. We keep the rentals in good shape and it attracts better tenants who usually keep the houses in good shape. We have definitely had problem tenants, who moved out in the middle of the night, beat up a home, and even moved out of state, but the tax-saving benefits and financial benefits have been well worth the occasional hassles. In fact, it is hard to get wealthy without some type of real estate investments in your life.

My law practice was a collection of dogs and cats. I did have some very wealthy clients who only seemed to work a few days per month. I studied them closely. They all seemed to get wealthy either from the stock market or real estate or both. You can do likewise. There are hundreds of excellent books on real estate investing at the library. This is not intended to be one of them.

However, I hope to convey the importance of investing in real estate, if you desire financial abundance in your life.

TOP LANDLORD WAR STORIES

My wife and I have over 20 years' experience as landlords involving 14 rental properties, mostly residential, and a few commercial. What follows are our top 5 "war stories".

DISAPPEARING ACT

We interviewed a couple from Italy, with limited English-speaking skills and eventually signed a 1 year lease on a home. They paid a $900.00 security deposit and paid rent 2 months in advance. Two weeks later, they disappeared. The neighbors called us stating there were 4 cats hanging around the house that looked like they were starving (the tenants said they had no pets). After numerous telephone calls over the next week, we eventually entered the unit and it looked like they went out to dinner and never came back. Their furniture was there. Their clothes were there. Their personal property was there. The only thing missing was their car.

Over the next several weeks, we checked with the police, the post office and the neighbors and as far as we could tell, they simply returned to Italy. We called the Humane Society who took the cats and we were later told they found homes for the cats.

Eventually, we put their furniture and clothing out to the curb and what was not "garbage picked" was taken by the garbage men. We never saw or heard from them again and re-rented the house.

ATTEMPTED MURDER

We also owned and rented the house right next door to a lady in her 20's and again, we were informed there was a problem from the neighbor. (We find it helpful to befriend the neighbors and give them our telephone number who indirectly keep and eye on your rental properties and are a great source of information). Anyway, a neighbor called and said there were 8 police cars, a SWAT team and 2 ambulances at the property the previous night and an ambulance took one tenant away and the other tenant was arrested.

When we arrived at the property there was police "Do Not Cross" tape all around the property. It took several days to figure out the story, but as it turns out our tenant, a female, had invited her boyfriend to move in a few months earlier. (We do not visit our rentals if the tenant pays timely and does not call for maintenance). We learned they ended up having a violent drunken argument one night when the girlfriend learned her boyfriend had an interest in another woman. The girlfriend stabbed him in the stomach repeatedly with a steak knife! He was in the hospital and she was in jail!

Our tenant could not make bail and sat in jail for many months awaiting trial. Eventually, her mother came to the property and got her daughter's belongings and we re-rented the unit. We never found out what her punishment was, but the former boyfriend did survive.

I guess Shakespeare was correct when he wrote "Hell hath no fury like a woman scorned"!

DRUNKEN TENANT

Another time we had a vacancy and we were meeting potential tenants at the rental property. One man who was interested showed up in his taxi at 2:00 in the afternoon. He said he was on a break. As we were speaking with him it was obvious he was drunk and he smelled like he just left a brewery. He was telling us what a great tenant he would be and he makes plenty of money as a taxi driver and he would love to rent the house and in fact would like to make a deposit immediately. He had a large wad of papers in his hand as he was speaking and I asked him what they were. He handed them to me and said "see for yourself". I read them and they were an eviction lawsuit for unpaid rent! Needless to say, we did not rent to him. We also called the taxi company he worked for and the police to report his drunken driving.

REVOLVING TENANTS

This was a friends' rental property, but I saw it with my own eyes. The trouble started, as usual, with the tenant not paying rent. The tenant's phone no longer worked and the landlord, my friend, asked if I would go with him to visit the property. The house was an hour's drive away and when we arrived, it looked like someone was living there so we knocked on the door. A man answered, but it was not the tenant so we explained who we were and asked who he was. He said he and his wife were tenants and they had moved in 3 weeks ago and had paid a security deposit, first month's rent and last month's rent totaling $4,200.00! Their "landlord" was my friend's original tenant. We explained he did not own the home and the lease did not allow sub-letting and he would have to move. He refused and eventually the police came to the home. Initially, the police explained to the occupant they were "squatters" and would have to move out within 24 hours or be arrested. The occupant eventually produced a written "lease" he had signed with the original tenant. Once that written lease was shown, the police told my friend it was a "civil matter" and if he wanted the tenant and his wife out, he would have to file an eviction lawsuit. I helped my friend file an eviction lawsuit and it took 5 weeks to get a final hearing, but we showed up and explained to the judge what happened. The current occupant showed up and explained his version of the facts and showed the judge his "lease". The judge asked him for proof of having paid $4,200.00 and that's when things got interesting. The man first said he paid $4,200.00 in cash. The judge asked to see the receipt. The man said he did not have a receipt and then changed his story and said he paid by check. The judge asked for a copy of the check and the man said he did not have a copy with him. The judge asked the name of the bank where he had the checking account. The man said he could not remember. It was obvious to everyone in the courtroom the man was lying. The man changed his story yet again and said he paid with a money order. The judge asked for a copy of the money order and the man said he did not have a copy. The judge announced that he felt the man was committing perjury and that is a serious offense punishable by jail. The judge granted the eviction, but told the man to remain the courtroom because they were going to conduct a "contempt of court" hearing to see if he had committed perjury, but first the judge had to handle the rest of his docket which would take about 90 minutes. The man, about 40 years old, was crying when we left the courtroom. We took the eviction order to the house, but the man's wife had already moved most of their stuff out of the home. They must have known the end was near even before the final hearing. The wife left and we changed the locks. With hindsight, we figured the original tenant was friends with this couple and they cooked up the whole scheme so the couple could live rent free for as many months as possible.

We never did find out what the lying man's punishment was, but it is never a good idea to lie to a judge.

THE CLAMPETTS

This was also a friend's rental, one I will never forget. As usual, the tenant stopped paying rent and my friend started the eviction process. One day he received a call from the neighbor who said you will not believe what the tenant did. The neighbor refused to say anything further so my friend and I drove to the house. The house looked fine from the front so we walked around the house. The back of the house looked like something out of a movie. The tenant had used a chain saw and sawed a huge square out of the back of the home! It was approximately 15 feet by 15 feet square. You could see the inside of the house like it was a child's doll house. We found out from the neighbor the tenant then cut the large section of wood into smaller sections and put them on the sides and back of his pickup truck. The tenant then piled all his belongings into the pickup truck and drove back to Tennessee. The neighbor said it looked like the "Beverly Hillbillies" truck when he drove away. Adding insult to injury, the tenant took all appliances, window treatments, light fixtures and even took the electrical outlets out of the wall. My friend filed a claim with the homeowners' insurance company and eventually received about 70% of the cost to repair the home. He never tracked down his former tenant.

CHAPTER 14
READY CASH

Always have ready cash. Our method was Certificates of Deposit. We have over a half million dollars in CDs, which we keep adding to when they mature. Sometimes we only add a few hundred dollars, sometimes $1,000, but they grow exponentially if you add money when they mature. At the time of this writing, we have historically low interest rates on CDs. I do not care. Even if our CDs paid no interest, I would not put them into another investment. Every time a CD matures, the banker asks me, "Are you sure you do not want to see one of our people to perhaps get a better return on your investment?" My standard answer is, "If I had any more stockbrokers, I would be in the poor house."

When you have a bunch of CDs, you do not panic when the stock market drops 40% like it did in 2008. In fact, you welcome a drop in the stock market, because you are prepared to buy large blocks of quality stocks like Johnson & Johnson and IBM. If the stock market has a large drop when you have liquid assets like CDs, you are in a position to ride the stock market back up and beyond—exactly like the stock market did between 2008 and 2017. When you have ready cash, you are not in panic mode if the stock market goes down, but rather in a position of strength. That's how I got wealthy: CDs, the stock market, and real estate.

I made a lot of mistakes with real estate and the stock market, but even with the mistakes, I became a multimillionaire.

ALWAYS HAVE READY CASH

CHAPTER 15
SELL YOUR LAW FIRM

Finally, when you are ready to cash out, sell your law firm, which is a well-established procedure. It starts by looking at Rule 4-1.17, Rules Regulating the Florida Bar. I used a business broker (simply a realtor specializing in selling businesses) and paid him 10% of the sales price. Actually, the broker who sold my business was the third broker I hired and ironically, the first two specialized in selling law firms, but neither got the job done. The third had sold a few law firms fifteen years earlier, but had been selling twenty to thirty other businesses per year.

What selling price to ask? Like any other business, it depends on gross sales and net profits. A good rule of thumb: you can expect to sell your firm for two to three times the net profits of your business. For example, if your firm nets $200,000.00, you can expect to receive $400,000.00 to $600,000.00 as a sales price.

I trained the buyer for sixty days and remained "of counsel" for twelve months and it was a "win/win" situation. The buyer got an established law firm with a profitable track record and good procedures in place. He had assistance from the seller (me), and I received a tidy sum of money and was able to retire at 55 years old to pursue scuba diving, wave running, airplane flying, high altitude climbing, and travel with family and friends.

A WIN/WIN INDEED.

CONCLUSION

Everyone desires abundance. Everyone desires money. Even a five-year-old likes money. Everyone desires wealth. However, very few people study wealth.

How do you get good at anything? Study and practice. There is no big secret to wealth and abundance. The rules are simple and straightforward. But do not confuse simple with easy. It is not easy to delay gratification. It is not easy to save and invest religiously. It is not easy to develop the discipline to "save for a rainy day" and live below your means. It is fun to drive a flashy car and live in a "McMansion."

To become wealthy, you do not need to be parsimonious, but you do need to be frugal. All of life is habits. You can develop good ones (like exercise, reading daily, saving money) or bad ones (like happy hour, restaurants five nights per week, and four hours of television every evening). The choice is yours.

A PERSON DOES NOT STUMBLE TO THE SUMMIT OF MT. EVEREST.

Nobody gets there by accident. You plan and prepare. The same holds true for your life. Is it worth it? You bet it is!

COLLECTION LETTERS

EXAMPLE #1

December 14, 2017

Mr. John Smith
4332 Violet Ave.
Tampa, FL 33602

Re: Smith v. Smith
PAST DUE: $500.00

Dear Mr. Smith:

My bookkeeper tells me you owe $500.00 which is over 90 days past due.

Could you please remit $500.00 within the next 5 days?

If this presents a problem, please let me know.

Very truly yours,

Michael Moran

cc: Bookkeeping

MM/va

EXAMPLE #2

December 14, 2017

Mr. John Smith
4332 Violet Ave.
Tampa, FL 33602

Re: **Smith v. Smith**
              PAST DUE: $1,443.90

Dear Mr. Smith:

My bookkeeper tells me you owe $1,443.90 which is substantially past due. This firm believes that it provides quality legal services. In return, we expect clients to pay their invoices on a timely basis.

Please pay your outstanding invoice by Friday, July 17, 2017. You seem like a nice man and I wish we could represent you for free, but that is not possible. This office has expenses like any other business.

Please pay your outstanding invoice no later than Friday, July 17, 2017.

Very truly yours,

Michael Moran

cc: Bookkeeping

MM/va

EXAMPLE #3

November 25, 2017

Mr. John Smith
4332 Violet Ave.
Tampa, FL 33602

Re: Smith v. Bank/$2,742.90 Past Due

Dear Mr. Smith:

My bookkeeper tells me you owe $2,742.90 and portions of that invoice are over 6 months past due.

We have been getting good results for homeowners, including principal reductions in some cases and winning foreclosure cases where the bank cannot prove its case. However, we cannot continue defending the above lawsuit without being paid. I am willing to reduce your invoice to $2,000.00 provided it is paid by Wednesday, December 1, 2017.

Alternatively, we are willing to accept as little as $500.00 per month until your invoice is reduced to zero. If you are to make monthly payments over time we cannot reduce the amount owed. As a general rule, we do not accept payment plans on outstanding invoices. This firm believes that it provides quality legal services. In return, we expect clients to pay their invoices on a monthly basis.

If you can get an attorney to represent you for free or less than we charge, feel free to do to and have him or her file a Notice of Appearance by December 1, 2017. If you want us to continue to defend the above lawsuit, please remit at least $500.00 by December 1, 2017 and on the first of each month thereafter until your outstanding invoice is reduced to zero. That is the best we can do.

If we do not receive at least $500.00 by Wednesday, December 1, 2017, we will have no alternative but to file a Motion to Withdraw. Once we withdraw, you will be representing yourself in the above lawsuit. In that case, the bank can win in as little as 25 days. In fact, the bank attorney often does file a Motion for Summary Judgment once we withdraw and if that Motion is granted, the bank wins the case. Not only can you be forced out of the home, but the bank can get a deficiency judgment for the difference between the amount owed and the value of the house. If the bank gets a deficiency judgment against you, they can do mean things like seize your bank account, seize vehicles and any other non-exempt assets in your name. I do not want to see that happen to you so if you are not going to continue with us, I would strongly urge you to get another attorney to defend the above lawsuit.

In sum, please remit $500.00 by Wednesday, December 1, 2017 if you want us to continue defending the above lawsuit. That is the best we can do. Please understand this office has expenses like any other business.

Very truly yours,

Michael Moran

cc: Bookkeeping

MM/va